Psalms 1-37 taken from the New International Version
Comment by E M Blaiklock Photographs by Gordon Gray

SCRIPTURE UNION

Published by
SCRIPTURE UNION
47 Marylebone Lane London W1M 6AX

ISBN 0 85421 798 3

Books in this series
Book 1 Psalms 1-37
Book 2 Psalms 38-75
Book 3 Psalms 76-111
Book 4 Psalms 112-150

Designed by Tony Cantale

Printed in England by W.S. Cowell Ltd.,
Buttermarket, Ipswich

Book 2 ISBN 0 85421 832 7

Book 3 ISBN 0 85421 833 5

Book 4 ISBN 0 85421 834 3

1 LIKE A TREE

Blessed is the man
who does not walk in the counsel of the wicked
or stand in the way of sinners
or sit in the seat of mockers.
2 But his delight is in the law of the LORD,
and on his law he meditates day and night.
3 He is like a tree planted by streams of water,
which yields its fruit in season
and whose leaf does not wither.
Whatever he does prospers.

4 Not so the wicked!
They are like chaff
that the wind blows away.
5 Therefore the wicked will not stand in the judgment,
nor sinners in the assembly of the righteous.

6 For the LORD watches over the way of the righteous,
but the way of the wicked will perish.

The Exile probably prompted a deprived people to put their 'Songs of Zion' together (Psalm 137.3). Someone ordered and arranged the collection. It was probably he, perhaps Ezra, who wrote this beautiful web of words. It is a poem with balanced halves, interior rhythm of ideas, and a triple pattern in verse. It was a poet dedicating his best art to God.

Like the Beatitudes, the psalm begins with the question of man's quest for happiness, and answers with insight. Those who seek the will of God in life, who shun contamination, who fear man's deadly processes of moral decline, whose roots are deeply where they should be, are happy. The writer knew Jeremiah (Jeremiah 17.5-8).

Chaff and fruitful tree stand in striking contrast. Chaff was the wind-blown pest of threshing time, unstable, useless. The desert, like the avid world, pants for trees. Trees grow, chaff perishes. The imagery is vivid.

2 YOU ARE MY SON

Why do the nations rage
and the peoples plot in vain?
2 The kings of the earth take their stand
and the rulers gather together
against the LORD
and against his Anointed One.
3 'Let us break their chains,' they say,
'and throw off their fetters.'

4 The One enthroned in heaven laughs;
the Lord scoffs at them.
5 Then he rebukes them in his anger
and terrifies them in his wrath, saying,
6 'I have installed my King
on Zion, my holy hill.'

7 I will proclaim the decree of the LORD:
He said to me, 'You are my Son,
today I have become your Father.
8 Ask of me,
and I will make the nations your
inheritance,
the ends of the earth your possession.
9 You will rule them with an iron sceptre,
you will dash them to pieces like
pottery.'

10 Therefore, you kings, be wise;
be warned, you rulers of the earth.
11 Serve the LORD with fear
and rejoice with trembling.
12 Kiss the Son, lest he be angry
and you be destroyed in your way,
for his wrath can flare up in a moment.
Blessed are all who take refuge in him.

The collector began with a set of psalms which, if Psalm 3 gives a hint, follow the progress of David's retreat before rebel Absalom. Long 'complacent in Zion' (Amos 6.1), David had forgotten his dimmed reputation, popular discontent, the need for vigilance. Had he not unified the land, extended its borders from Aqabah to beyond Damascus? Lulled by flattery, cushioned by an eastern court, Absalom's plotting had escaped him.

In sudden, stinging awareness, he found that the popular boy had betrayed him. Absalom was the fruit of a marriage forbidden by the Law. Judgment was home to roost. To be sure, the fickle mob followed vanity (1), but that made peril no less with hostile borderlands (1). Aware of danger, David was also aware of God. He could not forget that God had made him king. Hence a word with wider, later meaning (2). The old David, the poet, the man of God, was reborn in disaster, and his poem assumes wider mystic meaning as trouble does God's work.

3 A STRONG SHIELD

O LORD, how many are my foes!
How many rise up against me!
2 Many are saying of me,
'God will not deliver him.' *Selah*
3 But you are a shield around me, O LORD,
my Glorious One, who lifts up my head.
4 To the LORD I cry aloud,
and he answers me from his holy
hill. *Selah*
5 I lie down and sleep;
I wake again, because the LORD sustains
me.
6 I will not fear the tens of thousands,
drawn up against me on every side.

7 Arise, O LORD!
Deliver me, O my God!
For you have struck all my enemies on the
jaw;
you have broken the teeth of the wicked.
8 From the LORD comes deliverance.
May your blessing be on your
people. *Selah*

The old guerrilla fighter came to life, too. David knew that he could not hold Jerusalem. He knew that his strength was in the old wilderness, which had protected him from Saul, in the sheeplands in which his support lay.

He abandoned Jerusalem, daring a flank march across the enemy's front, for Absalom was a mere twenty miles south at Hebron.

Perhaps he swung north-east over the hills, and this psalm marks the first tense morning of the march to safety. Its mood passes from agony over the vast threat (1, 2, 6), to surging confidence. The perils of the night were over (5). The small band of the faithful was safe. Safety was over the hills. It is always well in danger to retreat to an ancient source of strength, not to believe man but God, when despair looms (2, 3). David had sinned his glory away, but he had also written Psalm 51.

6 BE MERCIFUL . . .

O LORD, do not rebuke me in your anger
or discipline me in your wrath.
2 Be merciful to me, LORD, for I am faint;
O LORD, heal me, for my bones are in agony.
3 My soul is in anguish.
How long, O LORD, how long?

4 Turn, O LORD, and deliver me;
save me because of your unfailing love.
5 No one remembers you when he is dead.
Who praises you from the grave?

6 I am worn out with groaning;
all night long I flood my bed with weeping
and drench my couch with tears.
7 My eyes grow weak with sorrow;
they fail because of all my foes.

8 Away from me, all you who do evil,
for the LORD has heard my weeping.
9 The LORD has heard my cry for mercy;
the LORD accepts my prayer.
10 May all my enemies be
ashamed and dismayed;
may they turn back in sudden disgrace.

The alternation of day and night suggests that the psalm joins the earlier four as an utterance of the great retreat (6). If so, why the change of mood? In life exaltation is often succeeded by a reaction. If the guess is correct and the king's party have struggled across the jungle-choked river, they must be in the grim Jabbok Gorge, where Jacob fought the Guardian of the land.

David was a desperately weary man. He was also, as many a psalm shows, a man of volatile and changing moods. He knew the heights, and, like others who do, he knew the depths. He was also acutely sensitive to landscape, and the Jabbok, his valley pathway to the Mahanaim heights, was a gloomy glen. It gave him, no doubt, his image of 'the valley of the shadow of death'.

He caught, too, out of old story, the sense of Jacob's anguish in the face of a morrow which could be ruin. David's morrow could be precisely that. The remedy was prayer. Hence the dramatic change (8-10). He had 'prayed through,' as was once said. God does sometimes grant the soul 'a season of clear shining, to cheer it after rain'.

8 GOD'S MAJESTY

O LORD, our Lord,
how majestic is your name in all the earth!

You have set your glory
above the heavens.
2 From the lips of children and infants
you have ordained praise
because of your enemies,
to silence the foe and the avenger.

3 When I consider your heavens,
the work of your fingers,
the moon and the stars,
which you have set in place,
4 what is man that you are mindful of him,
the son of man that you care for him?

5 You made him a little lower than the heavenly beings
and crowned him with glory and honour.

6 You made him ruler over the works of your hands;
you put everything under his feet:
7 all flocks and herds,
and the beasts of the field,
8 the birds of the air,
and the fish of the sea,
all that swim the paths of the seas.

9 O LORD, our Lord,
how majestic is your name in all the earth!

This small lyric is one of five 'nature psalms'. Perhaps it dates from shepherding on the hills of Bethlehem. The skies in those less polluted days were like those visible only from a high-flying plane today, almost solid with constellations. The sight, said Byrd, describing the winter night in Antartica, was 'overwhelming evidence of a vast, pervading intelligence'.

Under the immeasurable mingling of endless time and space does man seem small, too insiginificant for the mighty Mind behind phenomena? Indeed no. Verse 5 literally and correctly translated runs: 'You have made him a little less than God.' A child is more wondrous than a dead and arid planet. A mind which contemplates such glory and measures it, or notes, 'how sweet the moonlight lies upon this bank', is more significant than a lifeless galaxy; this psalm more awesome than the stars.

9 A STRONGHOLD

I will praise you, O LORD,
with all my heart;
I will tell of all your wonders.
2 I will be glad and rejoice in you;
I will sing praise to your name, O Most High.

3 My enemies turn back;
they stumble and perish before you.
4 For you have upheld my right and my cause,
you have sat on your throne, judging righteously.
5 You have rebuked the nations and destroyed the wicked;
you have blotted out their name for ever and ever.
6 Endless ruin has overtaken the enemy,
you have uprooted their cities;
even the memory of them has perished.

7 The LORD reigns for ever;
he has established his throne for judgment.
8 He will judge the world in righteousness;
he will govern the peoples with justice.
9 The LORD is a refuge for the oppressed,
a stronghold in times of trouble.
10 Those who know your name will trust in you,
for you, LORD, have never forsaken those who seek you.

11 Sing praises to the LORD, enthroned in Zion;
proclaim among the nations what he has done.
12 For he who avenges blood remembers;
he does not ignore the cry of the afflicted.

13 O LORD, see how my enemies persecute
me!
Have mercy and lift me up from the
gates of death,
14 that I may declare your praises
in the gates of the Daughter of Zion
and there rejoice in your salvation.
15 The nations have fallen into the pit they
have dug;
their feet are caught in the net they have
hidden.
16 The LORD is known by his justice;
the wicked are ensnared by the work of
their hands. *Selah*

17 The wicked return to the grave,
all the nations that forget God.
18 But the needy will not always be
forgotten,
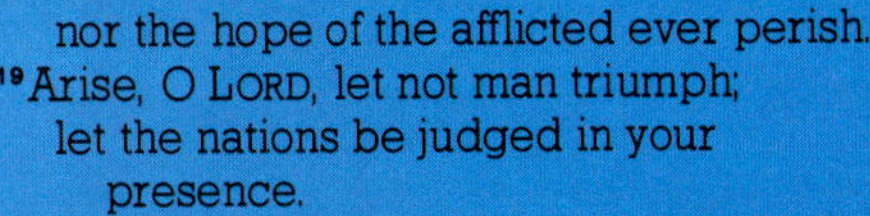
nor the hope of the afflicted ever perish.
19 Arise, O LORD, let not man triumph;
let the nations be judged in your
presence.
20 Strike them with terror, O LORD;
let the nations know they are but
men. *Selah*

The rabbi who arranged the psalms had reason to think that this confident hymn dated from David's second period of poetry when, the long retreat to the green and lovely uplands of Mahanaim over, he felt secure (9), certain of God's vindication (4, 10, 12, 13, 18), sure, as Joab gathered and drilled the loyal, that Absalom was already defeated (3, 16), and a triumphant return to Jerusalem certain (11, 14). He has no doubt that the hostile pagans on the borderlands would have been glad to intervene, and that it was the restraining hand of God which held them back (5, 15, 19).

The climax expresses a preoccupation of Old Testament writers, the vindication in heathen eyes of their God (9, 10). 'Those who know what thou art can trust in thee' (10, Moffatt). The climax recurs in the last verse. 'Made a little lower than God,' man is still man, who should bow in awe beneath 'the shadow of a great Right Hand'.

10 THE OPPRESSOR

Why, O LORD, do you stand far off?
Why do you hide yourself in times of trouble?

2 In his arrogance the wicked man hunts down the weak,
who are caught in the schemes he devises.
3 He boasts of the cravings of his heart;
he blesses the greedy and reviles the LORD.
4 In his pride the wicked does not seek him;
in all his thoughts there is no room for God.
5 His ways are always prosperous;
he is haughty and your laws are far from him;
he sneers at all his enemies.
6 He says to himself, 'Nothing will shake me;
I'll always be happy and never have trouble.'
7 His mouth is full of curses and lies and threats;
trouble and evil are under his tongue.
8 He lies in wait near the villages;
from ambush he murders the innocent,
watching in secret for his victims.
9 He lies in wait like a lion in cover;
he lies in wait to catch the helpless;
he catches the helpless and drags them off in his net.
10 His victims are crushed, they collapse;
they fall under his strength.
11 He says to himself, 'God has forgotten;
he covers his face and never sees.'

12 Arise, LORD! Lift up your hand, O God.
Do not forget the helpless.
13 Why does the wicked man revile God?
Why does he say to himself,
'He won't call me to account'?
14 But you, O God, do see trouble and grief;
you consider it to take it in hand.
The victim commits himself to you;
you are the helper of the fatherless.
15 Break the arm of the wicked and evil man;
call him to account for his wickedness
that would not be found out.

16 The LORD is King for ever and ever;
the nations will perish from his land.
17 You hear, O LORD, the desire of the afflicted;
you encourage them, and you listen to their cry,
18 defending the fatherless and the oppressed,
in order that man, who is of the earth,
may terrify no more.

The compiler sometimes grouped his psalms according to subject, and some words in Psalm 9 find echo in this true but repulsive picture of the godless man. The psalmist faces Habakkuk's dilemma of apparently prosperous evil (5). In pride the wicked persecute (2), boast arrogantly of their inner corruption (3), despise God with 'uptilted nose' (literally; the Hebrew for 'in his pride' [4])Contempt flows from his practised atheism (5, 6), a foul-mouthed (7), treacherous (8), violent (9) man. Worse, immunity seems given him (11).

It is natural that the good should cry out in agony (12-14), and shout for action (15), a cry which strangely seems to bring relief (16-18). Vision clears. Unburdening his hot heart, the suppliant sees the end, and is content to wait. Eternity surrounds this 'bank and shoal of time'. Time-bound, impatience comes too easily. But patience is good, prompts the searching of the heart, and grooms the good for eternity.

13 WAITING

How long, O LORD? Will you forget
me for ever?
How long will you hide your face from
me?
2 How long must I wrestle with my thoughts
and every day have sorrow in my heart?
How long will my enemy triumph over
me?

3 Look on me and answer, O LORD my God.
Give light to my eyes, or I will sleep in
death;
4 my enemy will say, 'I have overcome him,'
and my foes will rejoice when I fall.

5 But I trust in your unfailing love;
my heart rejoices in your salvation.
6 I will sing to the LORD,
for he has been good to me.

Here is dejection, words from David's days of exile. God seemed to have forgotten, not to care (1). Unanswered prayer made night and day heavy. The Septuagint puts 'every night' in verse 2 to balance 'every day'. No relief, no change, no cheer. It was like slow death, eyes glazing (3). Saul and his false henchmen were triumphant. He admits defeat but it was 'sorrow's crown of sorrow' to see the foe rejoice (4).

Then as though the very expression of despair had brought relief, old confidence arose. He has again the lilt of life's marching song. Something like reproach became praise, sun after thunder. Such is the object of prayer.

14 THE FOOL

The fool says in his heart,
'There is no God.'
They are corrupt, their deeds are vile;
there is no one who does good.

²The LORD looks down from heaven
on the sons of men
to see if there are any who understand,
any who seek God.
³All have turned aside,
they have together become corrupt;
there is no one who does good,
not even one.

⁴Will evildoers never learn –
those who devour my people as men eat
bread
and who do not call on the LORD?
⁵There they are, overwhelmed with dread,
for God is present in the company of the
righteous.
⁶You evildoers frustrate the plans of the
poor,
but the LORD is their refuge.

⁷Oh, that salvation for Israel would come
out of Zion!
When the LORD restores the fortunes of
his people,
let Jacob rejoice and Israel be glad!

The theme is general on the evil of the times, the common subject of this sombre group of psalms. Shallow fools look on the scene of wickedness and conclude that there is no God. They join the common corruption (1). Or is Francis Bacon right when he concludes that corruption comes first, and atheism follows to impart security (1)?

In three dramatic verses, the psalmist pictures earth as God sees it (2-4). He is concerned, yearning, and is to be involved—in Christ (2 Corinthians 5.19). The scene comes back to earth like the shifting visions of the Apocalypse, and in sudden terror the wicked discover that God was a member of the group they oppressed (Matthew 25.41-45). The Lord himself, Israel's Holy One, turns on those who have sought to organise society as if God didn't exist.

(The closing verse (7) does not date this psalm as post-exilic. It is like the closing verses of Psalm 51, added to the Psalter when it became the songbook of the second temple, but no less the word of God.)

15 THE UPRIGHT MAN

LORD, who may dwell in your sanctuary?
Who may live on your holy hill?

2 He whose walk is blameless
and who does what is righteous,
who speaks the truth from his heart
3 and has no slander on his tongue,
who does his neighbour no wrong
and casts no slur on his fellow man,
4 who despises a vile man
but honours those who fear the LORD,
who keeps his oath
even when it hurts,
5 who lends his money without usury
and does not accept a bribe against the innocent.

He who does these things will never be shaken.

Perhaps, like Psalm 24, this little hymn celebrates the restoration of the Ark to Zion. We turn from the denizens of corruption to find the clean man of God. Who shall be God's guest (1)? Ten characteristics follow, a sort of Decalogue. God has fellowship with sound, healthy men, who do not infect society with evil, men good at the core (the heart' [2]). They are without mendacity, treachery, spite. They do not listen to evil (3; 1 Corinthians 13.6—'love covers up'). They despise the doers of evil (Genesis 14.17-24), and honour not the high, the wealthy or any but those who reverence God (4). Such a man stands by his word, even to his detriment (4). He avoids unworthy or mean modes of life, such as money lending, so prone to spawn greed, rapacity (5). Such is the Jews' stainless man.

כתר
תורה
אנכי ה'
לא יהיה
לא תשא
זכור את
כבד את
לא תרצח
לא תנאף
לא תגנב
לא תענה
לא תחמד
לזכר נשמת
אמנו ואשתי היקרה בינה לאה שמ"ל
בת מנחם מנדל ז"ל
שנפטרה ביום ט"ז אלול תש
ת'נ'צ'ב'ה'

16 THE PATH OF LIFE

1 Keep me safe, O God,
for in you I take refuge.

2 I said to the LORD, 'You are my Lord;
apart from you I have no good thing.'
3 As for the saints who are in the land,
they are the glorious ones in whom is all my delight.
4 The sorrows of those will increase
who run after other gods.
I will not pour out their libations of blood
or take up their names on my lips.

5 LORD, you have assigned me my portion and my cup;
you have made my lot secure.
6 The boundary lines have fallen for me in pleasant places;
surely I have a delightful inheritance.

7 I will praise the LORD, who counsels me;
even at night my heart instructs me.
8 I have set the LORD always before me.
Because he is at my right hand,
I shall not be shaken.

9 Therefore my heart is glad and my tongue rejoices;
my body also will rest secure,
10 because you will not abandon me to the grave,
nor will you let your Holy One see decay.
11 You have made known to me the path of life;
you will fill me with joy in your presence,
with eternal pleasures at your right hand.

A beautiful expression of confidence and devotion from some high moment of David's experience. In a perilous world 'deliver us from evil' (1). 'Apart from you I have no good thing' (2). So David joins the blessed fellowship of the good (3; I John 3.14). It was a horrible world outside such a family, a world to be shunned (4). Like Joshua taking immediate stand (Joshua 24.15), David states his resolve (5). The Lord is his food and drink. His boundaries enclose a paradise (6), and God guides and governs the inner life (7), real as the friend who shields the sword-arm (8). The joy of it, the confidence, the hope (9)!

In the surge of it all, and in considering such a Lord, the psalmist's thought grasps the vast illogicality of death in a phrase Peter caught up at Pentecost (10, 11; Acts 2.25-28). God's guidance is not only specified direction, he accompanies the wayfarer (11).

17 KEPT BY GOD

Hear, O LORD, my righteous plea;
listen to my cry.
Give ear to my prayer –
it does not rise from deceitful lips.
2May my vindication come from you;
may your eyes see what is right.

3Though you probe my heart and examine me at night,
though you test me, you will find nothing;
I have resolved that my mouth will not sin.
4As for the deeds of men –
by the word of your lips
I have kept myself
from the ways of the violent.
5My steps have held to your paths;
my feet have not slipped.

6I call on you, O God, for you will answer me;
give ear to me and hear my prayer.
7Show the wonder of your great love,
you who save by your right hand
those who take refuge in you from their foes.
8Keep me as the apple of your eye;
hide me in the shadow of your wings
9from the wicked who assail me,
from my mortal enemies who surround me.

10They close up their callous hearts,
and their mouths speak with arrogance.
11They have tracked me down, they now surround me,
with eyes alert, to throw me to the ground.
12They are like a lion hungry for prey,
like a great lion crouching in cover.
13Rise up, O LORD, confront them, bring them down;
rescue me from the wicked by your sword.
14O LORD, by your hand save me from such men,
from men of this world whose reward is in this life.

You still the hunger of those you cherish;
their sons have plenty,
and they store up wealth for their children.
15And I – in righteousness I shall see your face;
when I awake, I shall be satisfied with seeing your likeness.

Some allege self-righteousness in verses 3 and 4. But David refers to the rituals of the Law. He had come to prayer with confession and proper preparation. The Lord's Prayer opens with a challenge to self-examination. No one can bypass: 'Thy will be done'. David is not hasty. He confesses frailty (5). He calls in trust (6, 7), in dire need of protection (8, 9).

This is probably a fugitive's prayer, lying hid with the valleys alive with Saul's commandos (9). He needs God's swift protection, rapid as the closing eyelid (8). The well-fed royal rangers were noisy in their probing of the hills (10), scanning each nook (11), tracking like lions (12). He lay listening, and in such peril only God could save from the pampered servants of the mad king (13, 14).

Again, as he concludes, vision seems to break through to a clear view of another life. With life as this psalm portrays it, a hunted, harassed, hungry hiding, it seemed madly unreasonable that this life should be all (15).

18 GOD'S ANSWER

I love you, O LORD, my strength.

2The LORD is my rock, my fortress and my
deliverer;
my God is my rock, in whom I take
refuge.
He is my shield and the horn of my
salvation, my stronghold.
3I call to the LORD, who is worthy of praise,
and I am saved from my enemies.

4The cords of death entangled me,
the torrents of destruction overwhelmed
me,
5The cords of the grave coiled around me;
the snares of death confronted me.
6In my distress I called to the LORD;
I cried to my God for help.
From his temple he heard my voice;
my cry came before him, into his ears.
7The earth trembled and quaked,
and the foundations of the mountains
shook;
they trembled because he was angry.
8Smoke rose from his nostrils;
consuming fire came from his mouth,
burning coals blazed out of it.
9He parted the heavens and came down;
dark clouds were under his feet.
10He mounted the cherubim and flew;
he soared on the wings of the wind.
11He made darkness his covering, his
canopy around him –
the dark rain clouds of the sky.
12Out of the brightness of his presence
clouds advanced,
with hailstones and bolts of lightning.
13The LORD thundered from heaven;
the voice of the Most High resounded.
14He shot arrows and scattered the
enemies,
great bolts of lightning and routed them.
15The valleys of the sea were exposed
and the foundations of the earth laid
bare
at your rebuke, O LORD,
at the blast of breath from your nostrils.

16He reached down from on high and took
hold of me;
he drew me out of deep waters.
17He rescued me from my powerful enemy,
from my foes, who were too strong for
me.
18They confronted me in the day of my
disaster,
but the LORD was my support.
19He brought me out into a spacious place;
he rescued me because he delighted in
me.

20The LORD has dealt with me according to
my righteousness;
according to the cleanness of my hands
he has rewarded me.
21For I have kept the ways of the LORD;
I have not done evil by turning from my
God.

[22]All his laws are before me;
I have not turned away from his decrees.
[23]I have been blameless before him
and have kept myself from sin.
[24]The LORD has rewarded me according to
my righteousness,
according to the cleanness of my hands
in his sight.

[25]To the faithful you show yourself faithful,
to the blameless you show yourself
blameless,
[26]to the pure you show yourself pure,
but to the crooked you show yourself
shrewd.
[27]You save the humble
but bring low those whose eyes are
haughty.
[28]You, O LORD, keep my lamp burning;
my God turns my darkness into light.

[29]With your help I can advance against a
troop,
with my God I can scale a wall.

[30]As for God, his way is perfect;
the word of the LORD is flawless.
He is a shield
for all who take refuge in him.
[31]For who is God besides the LORD?
And who is the Rock except our God?
[32]It is God who arms me with strength
and makes my way perfect.
[33]He makes my feet like the feet of a deer;
he enables me to stand on the heights.
[34]He trains my hands for battle;
my arms can bend a bow of bronze.
[35]You give me your shield of victory,
and your right hand sustains me;
you stoop down to make me great.

36You broaden the path beneath me,
so that my ankles do not turn over.

37I pursued my enemies and overtook
them;
I did not turn back till they were
destroyed.
38I crushed them so that they could not rise;
they fell beneath my feet.
39You armed me with strength for battle;
you made my adversaries bow at my
feet.
40You made my enemies turn their backs in
flight,
and I destroyed my foes.
41They cried for help, but there was no one
to save them –
to the LORD, but he did not answer.
42I beat them as fine as dust borne on the
wind;
I poured them out like mud in the
streets.

43You have delivered me from the attacks
of the people;
you have made me the head of nations;
people I did not know are subject to me.
44As soon as they hear me, they obey me;
foreigners cringe before me.
45They all lose heart;
they come trembling from their
strongholds.

46The LORD lives! Praise be to my Rock!
Exalted be God my Saviour!
47He is the God who avenges me,
who subdues nations under me,
48who saves me from my enemies.
You exalted me above my foes;
from violent men you rescued me.
49Therefore I will praise you among the
nations, O LORD;
I will sing praises to your name.
50He gives his king great victories;
he shows unfailing kindness to his
anointed,
to David and his descendants for ever.

The occasion is attested by 2 Samuel 22. It is David's language, vigorous, vivid in devotion; his life, perhaps, as it appeared on the morning of triumph, before the darkness fell on him and sin broke his joy.

He loved God, and the word for love is a strong one (1). He had been, like the sheltering crags, every kind of fortress (2). Into the tale of vast deliverance he wove the violence of the wilderness of Judea, storm, tempestuous gale, earthquake, gushing floods, rolling, flashing nimbus, hail, stabbing lightning . . . It was like life. Like a man rescued from the wrath of nature, God had drawn David from the tumult of events (3-19). The claim to righteousness (20-24) should not jar. David had not seen God in Christ (John 1.18). The triumphs of early kingship follow (28-45), with praise at the end. David had discovered a truth. It is worth waiting for God's time.

19 A TENT FOR THE SUN

The heavens declare the glory of God;
the skies proclaim the work of his hands.
2Day after day they pour forth speech;
night after night they display knowledge.
3There is no speech or language
where their voice is not heard.
4Their voice goes out into all the earth,
their words to the ends of the world.

In the heavens he has pitched a tent for the sun,
5which is like a bridegroom coming forth from his pavilion,
like a champion rejoicing to run his course.
6It rises at one end of the heavens
and makes its circuit to the other;
nothing is hidden from its heat.

7The law of the LORD is perfect,
reviving the soul.
The statutes of the LORD are trustworthy,
making wise the simple.
8The precepts of the LORD are right,
giving joy to the heart.
The commands of the LORD are radiant,
giving light to the eyes.
9The fear of the LORD is pure,
enduring for ever.

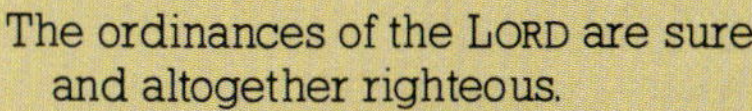

The ordinances of the LORD are sure
and altogether righteous.
10They are more precious than gold,
than much pure gold;
they are sweeter than honey,
than honey from the comb.
11By them is your servant warned;
in keeping them there is great reward.
12Who can discern his errors?
Forgive my hidden faults.
13Keep your servant also from wilful sins;
may they not rule over me.
Then will I be blameless,
innocent of great transgression.

14May the words of my mouth and the meditation of my heart
be pleasing in your sight,
O LORD, my Rock and my Redeemer.

This morning psalm could be a song of the Judean wilderness, the opal dawn (1), the tirelessly recurrent day and starry night (2), compassing a whole world (3), like a tent for the sun (4), rising now above the mauve Moab hills with a sudden, golden leap (5), to sweep across the sky (6). It is an entrancing vision of a poet at prayer.

And with such precision, so, too, the laws of the Spirit work (7), giving health to the soul, wisdom to the sincere, joy, life (8), clean minds, truth, goodness (9), sweetening life, enriching with true wealth (10). In sudden reverence, the psalmist feels warned (11) and unworthy of a God so magnificent in the garment of his creation, in his reality in the heart (12). Let man be humble (13), walk carefully, guard lips and thought (14).

We can use every word for a morning prayer. We can almost see the suppliant rise from his knees. The sun is high over the silver line of the Dead Sea. He faces the day. With his closing words we may, too.

20 A PROMISE OF VICTORY

May the LORD answer you when
you are in distress;
may the name of the God of Jacob protect
you.
2 May he send you help from the sanctuary
and grant you support from Zion.
3 May he remember all your sacrifices
and accept your burnt
offerings. *Selah*
4 May he give you the desire of your heart
and make all your plans succeed.
5 We will shout for joy when you are
victorious
and will lift up our banners in the name
of our God.
May the LORD grant all your requests.

6 Now I know that the LORD saves his
anointed;
he answers him from his holy heaven
with the saving power of his right hand.
7 Some trust in chariots and some in horses,
but we trust in the name of the LORD our
God.
8 They are brought to their knees and fall,
but we rise up and stand firm.

9 O LORD, save the king!
Answer us when we call!

A prayer for the king, as he rides forth on campaign. The Levites commit him to God in words he had written. The frontiers of strife, behind which Israel has always lived, called for such prayers.

It is a prayer of courage born of faith (1-3). Due sacrifice and preparation have been made, and the march begins in God's name (4,5). A single voice takes up the theme (6), perhaps the king's, full of confidence that prayer is heard. Then the choir resumes. The column about to march was imposing, but down to Edom or to the frontier beyond the Golan, it was not the floating banners (5) nor the rolling chariots which mattered. It was God who moved invisible beside. The fine little hymn ends with a cry of affirmation: 'God save the king', as the Septuagint and the Vulgate translate it.

21 THE KING'S JOY

O LORD, the king rejoices in your strength.
How great is his joy in the victories you give!
2You have granted him the desire of his heart
and have not withheld the request of his lips. *Selah*
3You welcomed him with rich blessings
and placed a crown of pure gold on his head.
4He asked you for life, and you gave it to him --
length of days, for ever and ever.
5Through the victories you gave, his glory is great;
you have bestowed on him splendour and majesty.
6Surely you have granted him eternal blessings

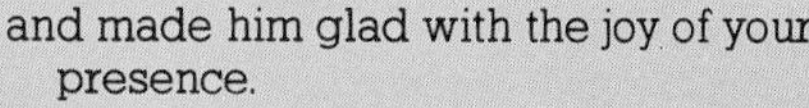

and made him glad with the joy of your presence.
7For the king trusts in the LORD;
through the unfailing love of the Most High
he will not be shaken.
8Your hand will lay hold on all your enemies;
your right hand will seize your foes.
9At the time of your appearing
you will make them like a fiery furnace.
In his wrath the LORD will swallow them up,
and his fire will consume them.
10You will destroy their descendants from the earth,
their posterity from mankind.
11Though they plot evil against you
and devise wicked schemes, they cannot succeed;
12for you will make them turn their backs
when you aim at them with drawn bow.

13Be exalted, O LORD, in your strength;
we will sing and praise your might.

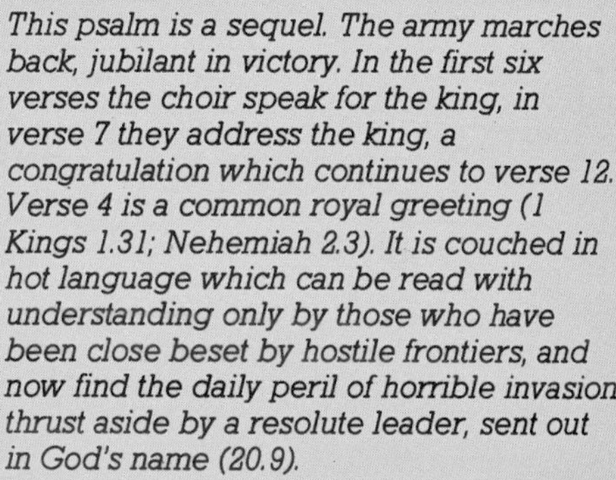

This psalm is a sequel. The army marches back, jubilant in victory. In the first six verses the choir speak for the king, in verse 7 they address the king, a congratulation which continues to verse 12. Verse 4 is a common royal greeting (1 Kings 1.31; Nehemiah 2.3). It is couched in hot language which can be read with understanding only by those who have been close beset by hostile frontiers, and now find the daily peril of horrible invasion thrust aside by a resolute leader, sent out in God's name (20.9).

Agonised prayer has been richly answered, and the last verse rescues the hymn from any charge that undue glory is given to the endeavour of a man. The victorious soldier recedes, and God alone remains. No nation can place hope elsewhere. Contrast this Hebrew ending with the appalling war-boasts of Assyria's inscriptions.

22 GOD'S SALVATION

My God, my God, why have you forsaken me?
Why are you so far from saving me,
so far from the words of my groaning?
2 O my God, I cry out by day, but you do not answer,
by night, and am not silent.

3 Yet you are enthroned as the Holy One;
you are the praise of Israel.
4 In you our fathers put their trust;
they trusted and you delivered them.
5 They cried to you and were saved;
in you they trusted and were not disappointed.

6 But I am a worm and not a man,
scorned by men and despised by the people.
7 All who see me mock me;
they hurl insults, shaking their heads:
8 'He trusts in the LORD;
let the LORD rescue him.
Let him deliver him,
since he delights in him.'

9 Yet you brought me out of the womb;
you made me trust in you
even at my mother's breast.
10 From birth I was cast upon you;
from my mother's womb you have been my God.
11 Do not be far from me,
for trouble is near
and there is no one to help.

12 Many bulls surround me;
strong bulls of Bashan encircle me.
13 Roaring lions tearing their prey
open their mouths wide against me.

14 I am poured out like water,
and all my bones are out of joint.
My heart has turned to wax;
it has melted away within me.
15 My strength is dried up like a potsherd,
and my tongue sticks to the roof of my mouth;
you lay me in the dust of death.
16 Dogs have surrounded me;
a band of evil men has encircled me,
they have pierced my hands and my feet.
17 I can count all my bones;
people can stare and gloat over me.
18 They divide my garments among them
and cast lots for my clothing.

19 But you, O LORD, be not far off;
O my Strength, come quickly to help me.
20 Deliver my life from the sword,
my precious life from the power of the dogs.
21 Rescue me from the mouth of the lions;
save me from the horns of the wild oxen.

22 I will declare your name to my brothers;
in the congregation I will praise you.
23 You who fear the LORD, praise him!
All you descendants of Jacob, honour him!
Revere him, all you descendants of Israel!
24 For he has not despised or disdained
the suffering of the afflicted one;
he has not hidden his face from him
but has listened to his cry for help.

25 From you comes my praise in the great assembly;
before those who fear you, will I fulfil my vows.
26 The poor will eat and be satisfied;
they who seek the LORD will praise him –
may your hearts live for ever!
27 All the ends of the earth
will remember and turn to the LORD,
and all the families of the nations
will bow down before him,
28 for dominion belongs to the LORD
and he rules over the nations.
29 All the rich of the earth will feast and worship;
all who go down to the dust will kneel before him –
those who cannot keep themselves alive.
30 Posterity will serve him;
future generations will be told about the LORD.
31 They will proclaim his righteousness
to a people yet unborn –
for he has done it.

This is prophecy, so stamped by Christ himself (Mark 15.27-34). It also reveals how prophecy is made. In some unrecorded hour of agony, David turned, as poets do, to poetry. He surrendered utterly his unbearable distress to God, and in a wild fervour of words he clutched at any image of horror to express his anguish. He had heard or seen the hideous invention of the Phoenicians, nailing a man to die in thirst and unspeakable pain on a cross, watched by crowds as insensitive as the wild herds of the Golan plateau, as a pack of dogs (12-19).

In such a passion of committal and reaching out for the eternal God did he write, that his words were snatched out of time and became eternal, and he wrote of a descendant after the flesh, dying for us. Such use can God make of surrendered experience.

23 THE GOOD SHEPHERD

The LORD is my shepherd, I shall
lack nothing.
2 He makes me lie down in green
pastures,
he leads me beside quiet waters,
3 he restores my soul.
He guides me in paths of righteousness
for his name's sake.
4 Even though I walk through the valley of
the shadow of death,
I will fear no evil, for you are with me;
your rod and staff,
they comfort me.

5 You prepare a table before me
in the presence of my enemies.
You anoint my head with oil;
my cup overflows.
6 Surely goodness and love will follow me
all the days of my life,
and I will dwell in the house of the LORD
for ever.

The psalm is placed here to follow, like the resurrection of Christ, the darkness of the last psalm's Calvary. It could follow Psalm 6, for surely the events of 2 Samuel 17.27-18.4 lie behind it. David has struggled out of the Jabbok gorge (4) and reached the green, watered pasturelands of Mahanaim (2). The shepherd-rancher met him regally, to play a part for God, and be his generous host (1,5). Perhaps David composed and sang the best-known poem of all time after the banquet.

It is exactly translated in the King James Version, even to the 'they' of verse 4. 'Your protecting club, your restraining crook, they comfort me, when nothing else does.'

Perhaps this is the royal psalmist's last utterance of poetry. He is certain now of returning to Jerusalem (6), but, outside his own mind, in a sweep of inspiration, he invades eternity in a glimpse of life everlasting. Such lights do 'surprise us on our way'.

24 THE KING OF GLORY

The earth is the LORD'S, and
everything in it,
the world, and all who live in it;
2for he founded it upon the seas
and established it upon the waters.

3Who may ascend the hill of the LORD?
Who may stand in his holy place?
4He who has clean hands and a pure heart,
who does not lift up his soul to an idol
or swear by what is false.
5He will receive blessing from the LORD
and vindication from God his Saviour.
6Such is the generation of those who seek
him,
who seek your face, O God of
Jacob. *Selah*

7Lift up your heads, O you gates;
be lifted up, you ancient doors,
that the King of glory may come in.
8Who is this King of glory?
The LORD strong and mighty,
the LORD mighty in battle.
9Lift up your heads, O you gates;
lift them up, you ancient doors,
that the King of glory may come in.
10Who is he, this King of glory?
The LORD Almighty—
he is the King of glory. *Selah*

The Ark is coming back to Jerusalem. David knew that it was but a symbol; the whole world was God's. Nevertheless it was another triumph of David's golden years when he brought the beautiful cabinet to the capital he had won from the Jebusites, Melchisedek's old town, and now a royal abode. One ringing voice called out the questions of verses 3, 8, 10 and the long, ordered procession of the Levites sang the answers.

It must have been a colourful sight as the column wound up the hill to the high city gates, the voices crying to an imaginary watchman to open the gates, to lift the arches if necessary. 'For whom? Who is this glorious visitor?' he asks. The reply is thunderous (10). There are gates still to open, barriers still to lift. For some we are ourselves responsible.

25 GOD'S WAY

To you, O LORD, I lift up my soul;
2 in you I trust, O my God.
Do not let me be put to shame,
nor let my enemies triumph over me.
3 No one whose hope is in you
will ever be put to shame,
but they will be put to shame
who are treacherous without excuse.

4 Show me your ways, O LORD,
teach me your paths;
5 guide me in your truth and teach me,
for you are God my Saviour,
and my hope is in you all day long.
6 Remember, O LORD, your great mercy and love,
for they are from of old.

7 Remember not the sins of my youth
and my rebellious ways;
according to your love remember me,
for you are good, O LORD.

8 Good and upright is the LORD;
therefore he instructs sinners in his ways.
9 He guides the humble in what is right
and teaches them his way.
10 All the ways of the LORD are loving and faithful
for those who keep the demands of his covenant.
11 For the sake of your name, O LORD,
forgive my iniquity, though it is great.
12 Who, then, is the man that fears the LORD?
He will instruct him in the way chosen for him.
13 He will spend his days in prosperity,
and his descendants will inherit the land.
14 The LORD confides in those who fear him;
he makes his covenant known to them.
15 My eyes are ever on the LORD,
for only he will release my feet from the snare.

16 Turn to me and be gracious to me,
for I am lonely and afflicted.
17 The troubles of my heart have multiplied;
free me from my anguish.
18 Look upon my affliction and my distress
and take away all my sins.
19 See how my enemies have increased
and how fiercely they hate me!
20 Guard my life and rescue me;
let me not be put to shame,
for I take refuge in you.
21 May integrity and uprightness protect me,
because my hope is in you.

22 Redeem Israel, O God,
from all their troubles!

Perhaps the presence of the Ark brought soul-searching (2, 4, 7, 11, 15, 17). Symbols of God's presence, and supremely the knowledge of God's nearness, should always stimulate such an exercise.

Prayer is a lifting of the soul (1), an affirmation of faith (2), a waiting on God (3). Guidance and understanding are our desperate needs (4), confidently asked for in the light of past mercy (5, 6), undeserved, but in mercy so often given (7). Such is his nature, his love (8-10).

'For the sake of your name' (11), means 'because you are what you are'. The words echo Psalm 23.3. To reverence God (12) is to be led by him, and know tranquility (13). His friendship is ours (14), and safety, if we are alert to his touch (15). The lonely and the troubled are his care (16).

In the last rush of words, the psalmist lists his afflictions (17-19), and their utterance brings peace. He will wait, if need be, but in faith (10-21). Verse 22 adapts the psalm for public worship—a Levite addition.

26 AN INNOCENT MAN

Vindicate me, O LORD,
for I have led a blameless life;
I have trusted in the LORD without
wavering.
2 Test me, O LORD, and try me,
examine my heart and my mind;
3 for your love is ever before me,
and I walk continually in your truth.
4 I do not sit with deceitful men,
nor do I consort with hypocrites;
5 I abhor the assembly of evildoers
and refuse to sit with the wicked.
6 I wash my hands in innocence,
and go about your altar, O LORD,
7 proclaiming aloud your praise
and telling of all your wonderful deeds.
8 I love the house where you live, O LORD,
the place where your glory dwells.

9 Do not take away my soul along with
sinners
or my life with bloodthirsty men,
10 in whose hands are wicked schemes,
whose right hands are full of bribes.
11 But I lead a blameless life;
redeem me and be merciful to me.

12 My feet stand on level ground;
in the great assembly I will praise the
LORD.

Self-examination continues. It was a blessed time in the first years of fulfilment, before the stresses of power and the temptations of success eroded the passionate desire to be right before God. His throne, like all the thrones of men, was fragile, and David knew that he held it in trust from a holy God, that he was responsible for those he gathered round him (4, 5, 9, 10).
God, that he was responsible for those he gathered round him (4, 5, 9, 10).

To ask God to search and try the heart (3), is a perilous prayer to pray, and dared only by those who truly seek his will. The royal psalmist asks for wholeness, and that can only be had by a soul redeemed. 'Tis mercy all, immense and free . . .' as Charles Wesley described it. Washed, cleansed, guided, only then can he hope to stand where the foot will not slip or stumble (11-12), on level ground, not sliding scree or sinking sand.

27 CONFIDENCE IN GOD

The LORD is my light and my
salvation –
whom shall I fear?
The LORD is the stronghold of my life–
of whom shall I be afraid?
2 When evil men advance against me
to devour my flesh,
when my enemies and my foes attack me,
they will stumble and fall.
3 Though an army besiege me,
my heart will not fear;
though war break out against me,
even then will I be confident.
4 One thing I ask of the LORD,
this is what I seek:
that I may dwell in the house of the LORD
all the days of my life,
to gaze upon the beauty of the LORD
and to seek him in his temple.
5 For in the day of trouble
he will keep me safe in his dwelling;
he will hide me in the shelter of his
tabernacle
and set me high upon a rock.
6 Then my head will be exalted
above the enemies who surround me;
at his tabernacle will I sacrifice with shouts
of joy;
I will sing and make music to the LORD.

7 Hear my voice when I call, O LORD;
be merciful to me and answer me.
8 My heart says of you, 'Seek his face!'
Your face, LORD, I will seek.
9 Do not hide your face from me,
do not turn your servant away in anger;
you have been my helper.
Do not reject me or forsake me,
O God my Saviour.
10 Though my father and mother forsake me,
the LORD will receive me.
11 Teach me your way, O LORD;
lead me in a straight path
because of my oppressors.
12 Do not hand me over to the desire of my
foes,
for false witnesses rise up against me,
breathing out violence.

13 I am still confident of this:
I will see the goodness of the LORD
in the land of the living.
14 Wait for the LORD;
be strong and take heart
and wait for the LORD.

This is an utterance of unclouded joy and faith triumphant. There is a sense of youth in the words. This is not the grief-clouded victory over Absalom, but some occasion of ecstatic success which made him remember the high moment when Goliath fell clattering before his sling (2; 1 Samuel 17.41-50) and all Philistia's army watched (3). 'Each victory will help you, some other to win', as David had once told Saul (1 Samuel 17.32-37). It had happened again on this occasion. High on some crag he looked from his refuge (5) and saw the frustrated foe far beneath (6). It was good to serve such a God. Life wilted if he seemed to turn away (9).

Verse 13 in the original is a subordinate clause which needs no amplification. David wrote: 'Unless I had believed . . . ' He added no main clause. Without the faith that God in goodness ruled the life, living could not be contemplated. Read the 'unless' clause very slowly, and fill in the main clause silently from personal experience. What might one do, be, become, without such blessedness?

28 GOD'S STRENGTH

To you I call, O LORD my Rock;
do not turn a deaf ear to me.
For if you remain silent,
I shall be like those who have gone down to the pit.
2 Hear my cry for mercy
as I call to you for help,
as I lift up my hands
towards your Most Holy Place.

3 Do not drag me away with the wicked,
with those who do evil,
who speak cordially with their neighbours
but harbour malice in their hearts.
4 Repay them for their deeds
and for their evil work;
repay them for what their hands have done
and bring back upon them what they deserve.

5 Since they show no regard for the works of the LORD
and what his hands have done,
he will tear them down
and never build them up again.

6 Praise be to the LORD,
for he has heard my cry for mercy.
7 The LORD is my strength and my shield;
my heart trusts in him, and I am helped.
My heart leaps for joy
and I will give thanks to him in song.

8 The LORD is the strength of his people,
a fortress of salvation for his anointed one.
9 Save your people and bless your inheritance;
be their shepherd and carry them for ever.

Anxiety, a whiff of doubt (1), open the prayer. Passionately David desires to be God's man, not to be swept away like the doomed, the wicked, the deceitful (3). A sudden fear has swept the heart lest the world's backwash of evil tear even the good man away; a fear lost in a moment, when prayer lightens the mind (6), and he sees that judgment falls only where judgment is due (4, 5).

Confidence returns like the clasp of a hand on the shield-strap. The faith which prays becomes the faith which possesses. The horizon widens, as prayer's landscape should. The king prays for his people (9).

29 GOD'S VOICE

Ascribe to the LORD, O mighty
ones,
ascribe to the LORD glory and strength.
2 Ascribe to the LORD the glory due to his
name;
worship the LORD in the splendour of his
holiness.

3 The voice of the LORD is over the waters;
the God of glory thunders,
the LORD thunders over the mighty
waters.
4 The voice of the LORD is powerful;
the voice of the LORD is majestic.
5 The voice of the LORD breaks the cedars;
the LORD breaks in pieces the cedars of
Lebanon.
6 He makes Lebanon skip like a calf,
Sirion like a young wild ox.
7 The voice of the LORD strikes
with flashes of lightning.
8 The voice of the LORD shakes the desert;
the LORD shakes the Desert of Kadesh.
9 The voice of the LORD twists the oaks
and strips the forest bare.
And in his temple all cry, 'Glory!'

10 The LORD sits enthroned over the flood;
the LORD is enthroned as King for ever.
11 The LORD gives strength to his people;
the LORD blesses his people with peace.

The uplands of the Judean wilderness, the tangle of David's hiding place, were a fine vantage-point from which to view the thunderstorms sucked down from Lebanon and Hermon (Sirion, [6]) into the hot pit of the Dead Sea. The nimbus clouds came in from the sea in enormous thunderheads, as Elijah saw them, roared among the cedar woods, swung south down the Jordan rift, and died down in the Kadesh wilderness.

David saw the storm's tumult as a vision of God's power. 'His chariots of wrath the dark thunder clouds form . . . ' So the tempests of the heart and the world's tumults roll on and die. To such a storm on Galilee Christ once brought calm (Mark 4.39). He can still quiet the stormy heart. He could quieten a gale-lashed world——if man would allow him.

30 GOD'S DELIVERANCE

I will exalt you, O LORD,
for you lifted me out of the depths
and did not let my enemies gloat over me.
2 O LORD my God, I called to you for help
and you healed me.
3 O LORD, you brought me up from the grave;
you spared me from going down into the pit.

4 Sing to the LORD, you saints of his;
praise his holy name.
5 For his anger lasts only a moment,
but his favour lasts a lifetime;
weeping may remain for a night,
but rejoicing comes in the morning.

6 When I felt secure, I said,
'I shall never be shaken.'
7 O LORD, when you favoured me,
you made my mountain stand firm;
but when you hid your face,
I was dismayed.

8 To you, O LORD I called;
to the Lord I cried for mercy:
9 'What gain is there in my destruction,
if I go down into the pit?
Will the dust praise you?
Will it proclaim your faithfulness?
10 Hear, O LORD, and be merciful to me;
O LORD, be my help.'
11 You turned my wailing into dancing;
you removed my sackcloth and clothed me with joy,
12 that my heart may sing to you and not be silent.
O LORD my God, I will give
you thanks for ever.

This song would appear to be the dedication hymn for the temple site, scene of David's unfulfilled dream. The writer has been 'lifted out' (1) from some such horrible prison as Jeremiah knew (Jeremiah 38.6-13). Or so it seemed, when some severe judgment had befallen him—perhaps the experience of 2 Samuel 24. It felt like some pit of abandonment (2, 3). But prayer found grace and a beautiful answer (4, 5).

The experience taught David a lesson. Like Jeshurun (Deuteronomy 32.15), he had grown arrogant, confident in self, not God. It is easy to grow lax and forget (6). He knew now, in fresh awareness, how fragile prosperity can be (7). Hence the salutary cry (8). And he has lost that fleeting vision of another life which we have seen granted to his deeper insights (9). Desperately he cries for aid (10), and wins it (11). His 'heart' is his God-consciousness, God's supreme gift, the part carnal man can maim and kill (12).

31 TAKE HEART

In you, O LORD, I have taken refuge;
let me never be put to shame;
deliver me in your righteousness.
2 Turn your ear to me,
come quickly to my rescue;
be my rock of refuge,
a strong fortress to save me.
3 Since you are my rock and my fortress,
for the sake of your name lead and guide me.
4 Free me from the trap that is set for me,
for you are my refuge.
5 Into your hands I commit my spirit;
redeem me, O LORD, the God of truth.

6 I hate those who cling to worthless idols;
I trust in the LORD.
7 I will be glad and rejoice in your love,
for you saw my affliction
and knew the anguish of my soul.
8 You have not handed me over to the enemy
but have set my feet in a spacious place.

9 Be merciful to me, O LORD, for I am in distress;
my eyes grow weak with sorrow,
my soul and my body with grief.
10 My life is consumed by anguish
and my years by groaning;
my strength fails because of my affliction,
and my bones grow weak.
11 Because of all my enemies,
I am the utter contempt of my neighbours;
I am a dread to my friends –
those who see me on the street flee from me.
12 I am forgotten by them as though I were dead;
I have become like broken pottery.
13 For I hear the slander of many;
there is terror on every side;
they conspire against me
and plot to take my life.

14 But I trust in you, O LORD;
I say, 'You are my God.'
15 My times are in your hands;
deliver me from my enemies
and from those who pursue me.
16 Let your face shine on your servant;
save me in your unfailing love.
17 Let me not be put to shame, O LORD,
for I have cried out to you;
but let the wicked be put to shame
and lie silent in the grave.
18 Let their lying lips be silenced,
for with pride and contempt
they speak arrogantly against the righteous.
19 How great is your goodness,
which you have stored up for those who fear you,
which you bestow in the sight of men
on those who take refuge in you.
20 In the shelter of your presence you hide them
from the intrigues of men;
in your dwelling you keep them safe
from the strife of tongues.

[21]Praise be to the LORD,
for he showed his wonderful love to me
when I was in a besieged city.
[22]In my alarm I said,
'I am cut off from your sight!'
Yet you heard my cry for mercy
when I called to you for help.

[23]Love the Lord, all his saints!
The LORD preserves the faithful,
but the proud he pays back in full.
[24]Be strong and take heart,
all you who hope in the LORD.

From such phrases as 'terror on every side', which occurs six times in Jeremiah, and some other turns of speech, some have thought that the prophet wrote this psalm. An old heading, however, sets it at the time David escaped into the southern desert of Maon.

It matters little. There are three movements—the cry of pain and the longing for some wilderness retreat (1-8); the desolate horror of loneliness when even friends turn away cruelly from such a spectacle of abandonment (9-13); the germination of trust and confidence (14-18), and the quietening of distress in God's enfolding care (19-22). The concluding two verses ring with confidence.

A good psalm to know by heart for life's darker days. The Lord quoted verse 5 on the cross. The New Testament and Christian hymns quote it frequently. It is good to weave Scripture into one's patterns of thought and follow its pathways when the mind is too weary to think.

32 FORGIVENESS

Blessed is he
whose transgressions are forgiven,
whose sins are covered.
2 Blessed is the man
whose sin the LORD does not count
against him
and in whose spirit is no deceit.

3 When I kept silent,
my bones wasted away
through my groaning all day long.
4 For day and night
your hand was heavy upon me;
my strength was sapped
as in the heat of summer. *Selah*
5 Then I acknowledged my sin to you
and did not cover up my iniquity.
I said, 'I will confess
my transgressions to the LORD' –
and you forgave
the guilt of my sin. *Selah*

6 Therefore let everyone who is godly pray
to you
while you may be found;
surely when the mighty waters rise,
they will not reach him.
7 You are my hiding place;
you will protect me from trouble
and surround me with songs of
deliverance. *Selah*

8 I will instruct you and teach
you in the way you should go;
I will counsel you and watch over you.
9 Do not be like the horse or the mule,
which have no understanding
but must be controlled by bit and bridle
or they will not come to you.
10 Many are the woes of the wicked,
but the LORD's unfailing love
surrounds the man who trusts in him.

11 Rejoice in the LORD and be glad, you
righteous;
sing, all you who are upright in heart!

This great penetential psalm could follow Psalm 51, but the compiler distributed the seven psalms of repentance throughout the Psalter. Three words for sin accompany two beatitudes (1, 2), for blessedness can only come with complete confession (3), and God presses hard on those he loves until all, all, is faced and put away (4, 5). Only then is forgiveness enjoyed and God

becomes a blessed refuge (6, 7). God's watching eye (8) is an awesome thought. 'The Lord . . . looked straight at Peter . . .' (Luke 22.61). To follow his glance is to see the path he indicates, and to sense his reproach or approval. It is a delicate partnership.

It is moving to find the joyous conclusion. Penitence is not remorse, and the sinner is free to forgive himself the sins for which God has forgiven him. The mercy of God rings the pardoned rebel like a fortress wall (10). Joy is called for, not lamentation.

33 HE GATHERS THE WATERS

Sing joyfully to the LORD, you
righteous;
it is fitting for the upright to praise him.
²Praise the LORD with the harp;
make music to him on the ten-stringed
lyre.
³Sing to him a new song;
play skilfully, and shout for joy.

⁴For the word of the LORD is right and true;
he is faithful in all he does.
⁵The LORD loves righteousness and justice;
the earth is full of his unfailing love.

⁶By the word of the LORD were the heavens
made,
their starry host by the breath of his
mouth.
⁷He gathers the waters of the sea into jars;
he puts the deep into storehouses.
⁸Let all the earth fear the LORD;
let all the people of the world revere
him.
⁹For he spoke, and it came to be;
he commanded, and it stood firm.
¹⁰The LORD foils the plans of the nations;
he thwarts the purposes of the peoples.
¹¹But the plans of the LORD stand firm for
ever,
the purposes of his heart through all
generations.

¹²Blessed is the nation whose God is the
LORD,
the people he chose for his inheritance.
¹³From heaven the LORD looks down
and sees all mankind;
¹⁴from his dwelling-place he watches
all who live on earth–
¹⁵he who forms the hearts of all,
who considers everything they do.
¹⁶No king is saved by the size of his army;
no warrior escapes by his great strength.
¹⁷A horse is a vain hope for deliverance;
despite all its great strength it cannot
save.
¹⁸But the eyes of the LORD are on those who
fear him,
on those whose hope is in his unfailing
love.
¹⁹to deliver them from death
and keep them alive in famine.

²⁰We wait in hope for the LORD;
he is our help and our shield.
²¹In him our hearts rejoice,
for we trust in his holy name.
²²May your unfailing love rest upon us, O
LORD,
even as we put our hope in you.

No author is named for this fine hymn. It is placed here because of its similarity in spirit to this section of the Psalter. The 'new song' means the utterance of a deeper awareness, a fresh and blessed insight into heaven's ways—God's love and faithfulness (4, 5), creation's 'awesome wonder' (6), the mighty deep (7), man's littleness before such majesty (8, 9). Paul was right (Romans 1.18-20).

And all such immeasurable might is behind his faithful purposes, against bent and distorted error (10, 11), and with the nation that observes his law, the theme of Isaiah's later writing (Isaiah 40-44). God watches the ebb and flow of empire, tramping armies, galloping cavalry and the pomp of fuming tyrants (13-17). And he observes his own (18, 19). History is not out of control, (Jeremiah 1). Patience (20), trust (21), hope (22) are all under his shield.

34 THE LORD IS GOOD

I will extol the LORD at all times;
his praise will always be on my lips.
2 My soul will boast in the LORD;
let the afflicted hear and rejoice.
3 Glorify the LORD with me;
let us exalt his name together.

4 I sought the LORD, and he answered me;
he delivered me from all my fears.
5 Those who look to him are radiant;
their faces are never covered with shame.
6 This poor man called, and the LORD heard him;
he saved him out of all his troubles.
7 The angel of the LORD encamps around those who fear him,
and he delivers them.

8 Taste and see that the LORD is good;
blessed is the man who takes refuge in him.
9 Fear the LORD, you his saints,
for those who fear him lack nothing.
10 The lions may grow weak and hungry,
but those who seek the LORD lack no good thing.

11 Come, my children, listen to me;
I will teach you the fear of the LORD.
12 Whoever of you loves life
and desires to see many good days,
13 keep your tongue from evil
and your lips from speaking lies.
14 Turn from evil and do good;
seek peace and pursue it.

15 The eyes of the LORD are on the righteous
and his ears are attentive to their cry;
16 the face of the LORD is against those who do evil,
to cut off the memory of them from the earth.

17 The righteous cry out, and the LORD hears them;
he delivers them from all their troubles.
18 The LORD is close to the brokenhearted
and saves those who are crushed in spirit.

19 A righteous man may have many troubles,
but the LORD delivers him from them all;
20 he protects all his bones,
not one of them will be broken.

21 Evil will slay the wicked;
the foes of the righteous will be condemned.
22 The LORD redeems his servants;
no one who takes refuge in him will be condemned.

The title attributes this psalm to a painful incident in David's life. Under Saul's persecution, so often borne heroically, David broke for one brief period, was tempted treasonably to aid the Philistines against his own people, and was saved from ultimate folly only because the Philistines naturally distrusted him. At one point he touched the depths of disgrace feigning madness to protect himself (1 Samuel 21.10-15).

The psalm runs on from the last verses of Psalm 33. In a gush of gratitude that he has been delivered from the deepest dishonour, David bursts into praise (1-3). The best a man can do with shame and self-abasement before his enemies is to turn the whole sorry situation into prayer, and hand the folly, the agony of it all, to God in full committal. Sin and stupidity can be transformed in those creative hands. So it comes about that David's disgusting conduct at the door of the Philistine chief gave the Bible and us such verses as 8, 14, 18, 22.

35 CONTEND FOR ME . . .

Contend, O LORD, with those who
contend with me;
fight against those who fight against me.
2 Take up shield and buckler;
arise and come to my aid.
3 Brandish spear and javelin
against those who pursue me.
Say to my soul,
'I am your salvation.'

4 May those who seek my life
be disgraced and put to shame;
may those who plot my ruin
be turned back in dismay.
5 May they be like chaff before the wind,
with the angel of the LORD driving them
away;
6 may their path be dark and slippery,
with the angel of the LORD pursuing
them.
7 Since they hid their net for me without
cause
and without cause dug a pit for me,
8 may ruin overtake them by surprise—
may the net they hid entangle them,
may they fall into the pit, to their ruin.
9 Then my soul will rejoice in the LORD
and delight in his salvation.
10 My whole being will exclaim,
'Who is like you, O LORD?
You rescue the poor from those too strong
for them,
the poor and needy from those who rob
them.'

11 Ruthless witnesses come forward;
they question me on things I know
nothing about.
12 They repay me evil for good
and leave my soul forlorn.
13 Yet when they were ill, I put on sackcloth
and humbled myself with fasting.
When my prayers returned to me
unanswered,
14 I went about mourning
as though for my friend or brother.
I bowed my head in grief
as though weeping for my mother.
15 But when I stumbled, they gathered in
glee;
attackers gathered against me when I
was unaware.
They slandered me without ceasing.
16 Like the ungodly they maliciously
mocked;
they gnashed their teeth at me.

17 O LORD, how long will you look on?
Rescue my life from their ravages,
my precious life from these lions.
18 I will give you thanks in the great
assembly;
among throngs of people I will praise
you.
19 Let not those gloat over me
who are my enemies without cause;
let not those who hate me without reason
maliciously wink the eye.
20 They do not speak peaceably,
but devise false accusations
against those who live quietly in the
land.
21 They gape at me and say,
'Aha! Aha!
With our own eyes we have seen it.'

22 O LORD, you have seen this; be not silent.
Do not be far from me, O LORD.
23 Awake, and rise to my defence!
Contend for me, my God and Lord.
24 Vindicate me in your righteousness, O
LORD my God;
do not let them gloat over me.
25 Do not let them think, 'Aha, just what we
wanted!'
or say, 'We have swallowed him up.'

26 May all who gloat over my distress
be put to shame and confusion;
may all who exalt themselves over me
be clothed with shame and disgrace.
27 May those who delight in my vindication
shout for joy and gladness;
may they always say, 'The LORD be
exalted,
who delights in the well-being of his
servant.
28 My tongue will speak of your
righteousness
and of your praises all day long.

The imagery of the desert guerrilla war he once had fought is vivid in the opening verses—the sudden seizing of weapons, some hard fight in a narrow pass, the attack or his own men scattering, and then pursuit on slippery hill paths treacherous in the fading light (1-6). Life is sometimes like that—'foemen leaning on our shield, and roaring on us as we reel'.

Yet all such battle was easier to bear than treachery, malicious tongues in the court of the half-mad Saul (7-11), and above all the base betrayal and the ingratitude of those to whom he had offered only friendship and fellowship in their sorrow. Ingratitude is a mean vice, sharper than the teeth of any winter wind. He who was 'tempted in every way, just as we are', knew this psalm and suffered, too, from false witnesses, base thanklessness, betrayal. The last noble words (27, 28) must be our prayer.

36 THE FOUNTAIN OF LIFE

An oracle is within my heart
concerning the sinfulness of the wicked:
there is no fear of God before his eyes.
2 For in his own eyes he flatters himself
too much to detect or hate his sin.
3 The words of his mouth are wicked and deceitful;
he has ceased to be wise and to do good.
4 Even on his bed he plots evil;
he commits himself to a sinful course
and does not reject what is wrong.

5 Your love, O LORD, reaches to the heavens,
your faithfulness to the skies.
6 Your righteousness is like the mighty mountains,
your justice like the great deep.
O LORD, you preserve both man and beast.
7 How priceless is your unfailing love!
Both high and low among men
find refuge in the shadow of your wings.
8 They feast on the abundance of your house;
you give them drink from your river of delights.
9 For with you is the fountain of life;
in your light we see light.

10 Continue your love to those who know you,
your righteousness to the upright in heart.
11 May the foot of the proud not come against me,
nor the hand of the wicked drive me away.
12 See how the evildoers lie fallen—
thrown down, not able to rise!

The first four verses are a perceptive description of a man who permits some sin to dwell at the deep core of his personality. The evil presence permeates his being, as evil, thus accepted, will. It colours speech and self-appraisal, deceiving its foolish host (2, 3), commanding his thought, and forcing surrender (4). The good man can stumble,

but loathes the enemy, who makes him slip.

The great piece of sacred poetry which follows (5-9), shows the gooa man's striving, looking up to the white summits, the high clouds, or over the immeasurable deep, symbols of the Godlikeness he covets (5-6). Less daunting imagery (7-9) shows him a satisfied guest in God's house of good. The stark contrast between the slimy creature at the beginning of the psalm, and the joyous servant at the end, prompts choice. Man can, of his free will, be either.

37 TURN FROM EVIL

Do not fret because of evil men
or be envious of those who do wrong;
2for like the grass they will soon wither,
like green plants they will soon die
away.

3Trust in the LORD and do good;
dwell in the land and enjoy safe pasture.
4Delight yourself in the LORD
and he will give you the desires of your
heart.

5Commit your way to the LORD;
trust in him and he will do this:
6He will make your righteousness shine
like the dawn,
the justice of your cause like the
noonday sun.

7Be still before the LORD and wait patiently
for him;
do not fret when men succeed in their
ways,
when they carry out their wicked
schemes.

8Refrain from anger and turn from wrath;
do not fret – it leads only to evil.
9For evil men will be cut off,
but those who hope in the LORD will
inherit the land.

10A little while, and the wicked will be no
more;
though you look for them, they will not
be found.
11But the meek will inherit the land
and enjoy great peace.

12The wicked plot against the righteous
and gnash their teeth at them;
13but the Lord laughs at the wicked,
for he knows their day is coming.

14The wicked draw the sword and bend
the bow
to bring down the poor and needy,
to slay those whose ways are upright.
15But their swords will pierce their own
hearts,
and their bows will be broken.

16Better the little that the righteous have
than the wealth of many wicked;
17for the power of the wicked will be
broken,
but the LORD upholds the righteous.

18The days of the blameless are known to
the LORD,
and their inheritance will endure for
ever.
19In times of disaster they will not wither;
in days of famine they will enjoy plenty.

20But the wicked will perish:
the LORD's enemies will be like the
beauty of the fields,
they will vanish – vanish like smoke.

21The wicked borrow and do not repay,
but the righteous give generously;
22those the LORD blesses will inherit the
land,
but those he curses will be cut off.

23The LORD delights in the way of the man
whose steps he has made firm;
24though he stumble, he will not fall,
for the LORD upholds him with his hand.

25I was young and now I am old,
yet I have never seen the righteous
forsaken,
or their children begging bread.
26They are always generous and lend
freely;
their children will be blessed.
27Turn from evil and do good;
then you will always live securely.
28For the LORD loves the just
and will not forsake his faithful ones.

They will be protected for ever,
but the offspring of the wicked will be
cut off;

[29]the righteous will inherit the land
and dwell in it for ever.

[30]The mouth of the righteous man utters
wisdom,
and his tongue speaks what is just.
[31]The law of his God is in his heart;
his feet do not slip.

[32]The wicked lie in wait for the righteous,
seeking their very lives;
[33]but the LORD will not leave them in their
power
or let them be condemned when
brought to trial.

[34]Wait for the LORD
and keep his way.
He will exalt you to possess the land;
when the wicked are cut off, you will
see it.

[35]I have seen a wicked and ruthless man
flourishing like a green tree in its native
soil,
[36]but he soon passed away and was no
more;
though I looked for him, he could not be
found.

[37]Consider the blameless, observe the
upright;
there is a future for the man of peace.
[38]But all sinners will be destroyed;
the future of the wicked will be cut off.

[39]The salvation of the righteous comes from
the LORD;
he is their stronghold in time of trouble.
[40]The LORD helps them and delivers them;
he delivers them from the wicked and
saves them,
because they take refuge in him.

With repetitive cadences, this psalm proclaims the blessedness of the deeply committed life. The psalmist takes up the theme of Psalm 36, and shows the absurdity of fretting over evil that cannot last (1, 2, 34, 35, 36). The mood is quietness and confidence, and the good man's power over surrounding evil (9, 12, 13, 16, 28).

The armour is tranquil trust (3) and service that delights (4)—not the dour obedience of the Prodigal's brother (Luke 15.29), nor of those whom Malachi rebukes (Malachi 3.14). Such faithful ones shall be given what their most sacred aspirations covet ('desires of the heart'). They shall receive what God's will knows is best (5). In rest and patient waiting (7, 34)—but not passive, inactive waiting (3—'do good')—is the soul's tranquility. The good man lives on another plane; a new dimension of being is his dwelling place. He is 'part of the permanent'. (See JB Phillips on 1 John 2.17)